STEP-BY-STEP

Creative Houseplants

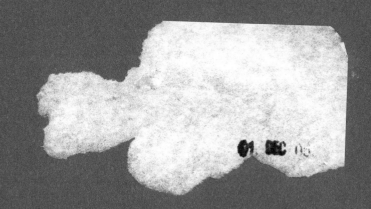

01 DEC 09

STEP-BY-STEP

Creative
Houseplants

Andrew Clinch

LORENZ BOOKS

LONDON • NEW YORK • SYDNEY • BATH

This edition first published in the UK in 1997 by Lorenz Books

Lorenz Books is an imprint of
Anness Publishing Limited
Hermes House
88-89 Blackfriars Road
London SE1 8HA

ISBN 1 85967 344 9

A CIP catalogue record is available from the British Library

Publisher: Joanna Lorenz
Project Editor: Joanne Rippin
Designer: Peter Laws/Blackjacks
Photography: John Freeman

Additional projects supplied by Clare Bradley (p 42)
and Ken Norman (p 50)

Printed and bound in Hong Kong

1 3 5 7 9 10 8 6 4 2

CONTENTS

INTRODUCTION

Today we can enjoy a wider range of houseplants than ever before. Gone are the days when most people chose between rubber plants (*Ficus elastica*) and Swiss cheese plants (*Monstera deliciosa*), when a flowering houseplant was probably either a geranium (pelargonium) or a Busy Lizzie (impatiens), and it was a rarity to find a gardenia or a bougainvillea in the local garden centre.

Now you can go to almost any garden centre of even modest size and buy yourself an orchid or a bird-of-paradise flower (strelitzia) – not to mention the now almost commonplace exotic bougainvillea or marvellously fragrant gardenia. If the curious fascinates you, there will be a range of insectivorous plants to choose from, voodoo lilies (you need a strong stomach for these – their strange flowers stink of rotting meat!), or perhaps air plants (tillandsia), which don't even need soil to grow in.

If you want to garden indoors on a budget, you could even pot up a few plants from the garden – such as hostas or astilbes – to grow as short-term pot plants. Or grow annuals from seed, such as Busy Lizzies or Persian violets (*Exacum affine*).

Have fun with your houseplants. If you can bring yourself to regard some of them as you might long-lasting cut flowers, rather than expecting them to last for years, they will give you immense pleasure. Move them around, experiment, try different pots and a range of ways of displaying your plants. And don't be afraid to try something new or unusual – especially if it is inexpensive.

Pick of the Bunch

Flowering houseplants are usually more difficult than foliage plants to keep long-term (some are annuals and have to be discarded when flowering is over). But they add brilliance and colour that even the boldest foliage plants find difficult to match, and some have that magical extra ingredient: fragrance. A few flowering plants are available throughout the year (chrysanthemums, kalanchoës and African violets are examples), but most flower in a particular season. This is no bad thing because it prevents your displays becoming predictable or boring.

Here is a small selection of the most reliable and widely available flowering pot-plants. You will find many more, and it is always worth keeping your eye open for something unusual to try.

Stephanotis floribunda

Streptocarpus

Tillandsia cynea

Gardenia

Exacum affine

Vriesea

Hydrangea

Achimenes

Clivia miniata

Pelargonium, Regal

Jasminum polyanthum

Primula obconica

Saintpaulia

Beloperone guttata (syn. Justicia brandegeeana)

Chrysanthemum

Codiaeum

Anthurium scherzercrianum

Begonia (Elatior type)

Kalanchoë

Azalea (rhododendron)

Aechmea fasciata

Fantastic Foliage

Foliage plants need not be dull. There are many variegated kinds, and some leaves are more colourful than many flowers – and much longer-lasting. But don't dismiss green foliage plants – their interest lies in their contrasting textures and shapes, and there are hundreds of different shades of green! Plants grown for their leaves will form the backbone of most arrangements and groupings. They can also form a backdrop for the flowers, rather as trees and shrubs do in the garden. The foliage plants illustrated here are just a few of the many hundreds that are readily available, but they combine reliability with beauty and should form the backbone of any collection.

Yucca

Asparagus densiflorus sprengeri

Sansevieria trifasciata 'Laurentii'

Aglaonema 'Silver Queen'

Tillandsias (air plants)

Hedera helix (variegated variety)

Chlorophytum comosum 'Vittatum'

Ficus pumila 'Sonny'

Asplenium nidus

Maranta leuconeura var. kerchoveana

Ficus benjamina 'Starlight'

Dieffenbachia picta 'Camilla'

Schefflera arboricola 'Aurea'

Monstera deliciosa

Howea belmoreana

Fatsia japonica

Begonia rex

Philodendron scandens

Dracaena marginata

Maranta leuconeura var. erythroneura (sometimes sold as Maranta tricolor)

Syngonium podophyllum

Chamaedorea elegans

Shopping for Houseplants

This may appear to be the easiest part of growing houseplants! But if you've ever tried to obtain good specimens of specific plants just when you want them, you'll know it isn't so easy. Plants are living, perishable things, and supplies often fluctuate widely according to season and what the commercial growers decide to market. You will always find some of the basic foliage plants, but novel or less common plants may be grown only in small quantities or for a limited time. But this all adds to the fun of hunting for plants.

1 Market stalls and outdoor displays in front of shops can look tempting, and the plants may be less expensive than from a garden centre or florist, but be cautious. Buying in the summer (unless it is very windy) is a fairly safe bet, but at other times avoid plants that are sensitive to cold. Plants like poinsettias and codiaeums may look good, even when you get them home, but the chill may cause them to turn yellow or drop their leaves prematurely. Don't expect to find the more exotic plants here, but you should be able to obtain the most common sorts – which are often the most reliable anyway.

What's Up the Sleeve

Beware of plants in sleeves or bags. These can afford useful protection on the way home, but make sure they don't hide diseases or other problems. Slip the plant you want to buy out of its sleeve and check for signs of rot or fungal diseases, as well as pests, any of which can multiply rapidly in such protected conditions.

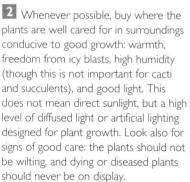

2 Whenever possible, buy where the plants are well cared for in surroundings conducive to good growth: warmth, freedom from icy blasts, high humidity (though this is not important for cacti and succulents), and good light. This does not mean direct sunlight, but a high level of diffused light or artificial lighting designed for plant growth. Look also for signs of good care: the plants should not be wilting, and dying or diseased plants should never be on display.

3 Make a point of looking beneath the pot if you think the plant looks starved or root-bound (when the potting soil is filled with roots). It is normal for some roots to be growing through the bottom of the pot if capillary matting has been used for watering, but masses of long roots are an indication that the plant should probably have been repotted. It may be starved or checked in its growth.

4 Always check the plant for signs of pests and diseases. Make a point of turning over one or two of the leaves – pests may be lurking out of sight.

5 Timing is everything with flowering plants. Don't buy a plant in full bloom if you can choose one with just a few flowers out but lots of buds still to open. You may get several extra weeks of pleasure if you buy a plant just coming into flower rather than one that is already at its peak.

Tools and Equipment

You can look after your houseplants without any special tools. An old kitchen fork and spoon are amazingly versatile, and some real enthusiasts manage with a jug from the kitchen cupboard instead of a proper watering-can. But the right tools do make the jobs easier, and usually more pleasant. The tools described here won't cost much and may save a lot of frustration. Take particular care over the choice of a watering-can and a mister – both should be in daily use, so don't skimp on these.

Canes (stakes); usually made from bamboo, used for supporting plants. Dibber; a tool used for making a hole in soil or potting soil. Fertilizer; food for plants which comes in various forms. Knife; useful for taking cuttings and other indoor gardening tasks. Leaf shines; products for putting a shine on glossy leaves. Leaf wipes; tissue-type leaf shine. Mister; a sprayer producing a fine mist. Insecticide; for pest control. Insecticidal plant pins; insecticide-impregnated strips to push into potting soil. Raffia; a natural tying material. Rooting hormone; stimulates root formation on cuttings. Scissors; useful for cutting ties and deadheading etc. Water indicator; indicates moisture level in soil. Watering-can, indoor; one with a long, narrow spout for precision watering. Wire, plastic-covered; plastic coating protects stems.

selection of pots of different sizes

leaf wipes

indoor watering-can

leaf shine

mister

insecticide

raffia

water indicator

plastic-covered wire

fertilizers (liquid, tablets, pellets and sticks)

insecticidal plant pin

hormone rooting powder

small dibber

sharp knife

scissors

canes (stakes)

Soil Sense

Potting soils sound exceedingly boring, but treat this apparently mundane subject with respect. The use of an appropriate potting soil (or other medium, for nowadays soil or loam may not be an ingredient) can make all the difference to successful indoor gardening. Get it wrong, and you could even kill your plant. A potting soil is much more than something that serves as an anchor – it provides vital nutrients essential for growth, and acts as a reservoir for moisture. Loam-based (soil-based) potting soil is heavier and less pleasant to handle than peat-based versions, but it may be the best choice for some plants. Tall or large plants that tend to be top-heavy may benefit from the extra weight in the pot. Some plants, including most succulents, benefit from the good drainage compared with peat-based potting soils and other loam substitutes, and these soils hold a better reserve of nutrients. Peat-based mixtures are light and easy to handle, but usually require supplementary feeding after a month or so. They can vary greatly in quality, so when you have found one that is satisfactory, it's a good idea to stick to it.

Orchid mixtures are unlike any others that you will use. They are free-draining and contain no loam (soil). Bark is a common ingredient. The orchids for which they are used grow mainly on trees in the litter that forms in crevices and the angles between branches, and that is what these formulations seek to replicate. Cactus soils are very free-draining, and will contain plenty of grit or other material to ensure the roots don't become waterlogged. Ericaceous potting soils are for acid-loving plants. You can't tell that a potting soil is ericaceous simply by looking at it – but lime or other alkaline materials are not used in the mixture, and the pH is more acidic than in normal soils.

Water-absorbing granules are sometimes used as an additive. They swell when wet and hold many times their own weight of water. They can be useful if you are often away for a few days and find it difficult to water regularly.

peat (peat-moss) potting soil

loam-based (soil-based) potting mixture

orchid mixture

cactus mixture

fine gravel

chipped bark

expanded clay granules

Repotting

Repotting will help to keep most of your plants growing vigorously, though some prefer to be kept in a relatively small pot. Bromeliads and plants that normally grow in little or no soil do not require frequent repotting, but most plants benefit from being moved into a larger pot at least once a year.

BE PREPARED

Water the plant about an hour before repotting, then remove it from the pot. Sometimes it will come free with a gentle pull, otherwise invert it, holding your fingers over the surface of the potting soil, and tap the edge of the pot on a hard surface. This usually dislodges the root-ball.

1 Choose a new pot one size larger for a slow-growing plant, two sizes larger for a fast grower. Place a layer of potting soil in the base. If you are using a clay pot, cover the hole in the bottom with crocks (pieces of broken clay pot) – if you don't have any, use broken polystyrene tile or chipped bark.

2 Estimate how much potting soil you need to add to raise the root-ball to about 1 cm (½ in) below the rim. Try it for size – you may have to add a little more potting soil, or remove some. Whenever possible, use the same type of potting soil as that in the original pot (peat-based or loam-based for example).

3 Once you have the height right, simply place the root-ball in the centre of the new pot and trickle the potting soil into the gap around the edge. Turn the pot as you work. If the roots were tightly wound around the edge of the root-ball, tease some of them out to encourage rooting into the new potting soil.

4 Gently firm the potting soil with your fingers. Add a little more if necessary. Leave space for watering. Unless the pot is small, leave about 1 cm (½ in) between the surface and the rim. Be sure to water in thoroughly.

WHEN TO REPOT

If there are lots of thick roots growing through the bottom of the pot, it's time to pot on into a larger size. If growth seems poor and the plant has been in its container for many months, lift or knock it out of the pot and examine the root-ball. If the potting soil is a dense mass of roots, or long roots are winding around the edge of the pot, it's a good idea to consider moving up a pot size or two. If the pot is already large, annual repotting may not be feasible. Instead, remove the top 2.5 cm (1 in) of the potting soil and replace with fresh.

Feeding Facts

If you want lush and healthy houseplants you must feed them. They may hang on to life for years without it, but feeding is what makes them grow. The cost is negligible in comparison with buying new plants, and modern slow-release fertilizers mean that it isn't even a chore.

3 Fertilizer tablets or pellets may be more difficult to insert. If necessary, make a small hole of appropriate size with a pencil or small stick, insert the fertilizer then push it in further with the pencil.

1 The easiest way to feed your houseplants is with a slow-release or controlled-release fertilizer. There are many kinds: some come as granules, others as pellets or tablets, or in sachets that you place beneath the plant in the pot. Slow-release fertilizers feed the plant steadily over a period of months, controlled-release types release the fertilizer only when the potting soil is above a temperature suitable for the active growth of most plants. The latter is useful outdoors, but indoors it makes little difference which you choose. Granules can be mixed with the potting soil before potting; pellets can be pushed into the soil around an established plant.

2 Fertilizer sticks are simply pushed into the potting soil. Just insert a new one at the frequency recommended by the manufacturer.

SEE FOR YOURSELF

The best way to convince yourself of the benefits of feeding is to set up a small experiment. Take two plants – perhaps cuttings you have rooted yourself, then you'll know that the potting soil does not already contain a slow-release fertilizer – and add a dose of slow-release plant food to one of them. Be sure to keep the plants side by side and give them identical care. The chances are you'll be amazed at the difference a month or so later.

4 Granular or powder fertilizers are more difficult to use for houseplants. You need to calculate the amount needed for a pot, then carefully stir it into the surface – an old kitchen fork is useful for this.

5 Liquid feeds are still popular, and make it easier than with slow-release products to stop feeding when the plant reaches a resting phase. Some are designed to be applied at a very weak rate with regular watering, others at a stronger application rate but only perhaps once a week or fortnight. Always follow the manufacturer's advice.

Wash and Brush Up

Give your plants a wash occasionally – or if they have hairy leaves, a brush – to keep them looking smart. There is dust in even the cleanest house, and you may not realize how lack-lustre this makes your plants look until you clean them.

1 Plants with large, glossy leaves, such as *Ficus elastica*, *F. lyrata*, crotons (codiaeum) and palms, can be wiped clean. Commercially produced leaf wipes are convenient to use, but check that they don't carry a warning against using them on certain plants.

2 Dead flowers will mar your plants. Remove them as soon as they fade. It takes only a moment, yet this simple task will keep your plants looking smart.

3 Sooner or later, leaves fall from all plants. Pick them up before they start to rot and encourage diseases. Dead leaves lying around will detract from the beauty of your plants. Leaves will naturally turn yellow or die on plants that die down for a resting period – such as cyclamen – but pull them off regularly so your plants don't look neglected.

4 Hairy leaves are much more difficult to clean. Try brushing them carefully with a soft paintbrush.

STANDING IN THE RAIN

Plants with small glossy leaves may have too many of them to make the leaf-wipes a sensible option. Try standing the plants outside in a shower of light rain in the summer, or spray them with water. In winter, plants small enough to be handled in this way can simply have their leaves swished gently in a bowl of tepid water. Don't do this, however, if the leaves are delicate or hairy.

Watering Wisdom

One has to face up to it – unless you use self-watering containers or a hydroponic system, watering is a chore. It's also probably the biggest cause of plant losses apart from pests and diseases. Try to get into a routine with watering. Check your plants at least daily – even if they don't require water, it gives you an opportunity to keep an eye open for early signs of any other problems.

1 Small water indicator flags that can be left in the pot are less time-consuming to use than meter probes, which you have to push into each pot each day. The indicators change colour according to the moisture content.

2 It's a good idea to get into the habit of feeling the surface of the soil. This tells you a lot about how moist the potting soil is, and it's surprising how quickly you learn to judge when to water.

3 Most people use a watering-can, with excellent results. But choose one with a long, narrow spout so that you can control the flow easily. You want the water around the roots, not over the leaves or on your table or windowsill.

4 Don't allow the pot to stand in surplus water. Many plants will succumb if the potting soil remains waterlogged for long periods.

INDIVIDUAL NEEDS

Many houseplants are killed by overwatering. Some plants will require watering daily, others perhaps once or twice a week. In winter, some may not need water for weeks on end. Always treat the needs of plants individually. Don't water just because a moisture meter or indicator tells you the potting soil is dry. Cacti and succulents resting during winter, for example, should not be kept constantly moist.

MOISTURE METERS

You can buy moisture meters that will indicate whether the potting soil is moist or dry. These are useful if you are a beginner, but if you have a lot of plants it will make watering even more of a chore if you have to go around a lot of plants pushing a probe into each pot.

Growing in Water

Hydroponic culture (growing in water) can be very successful, and is very popular in some countries. To make life simple, use a proprietary kit that includes aggregate and special fertilizer as well as a water-level indicator. You will need to buy special ion-exchange fertilizers designed for hydroponics, which will provide sufficient nutrients for many months.

1 Choose a decorative watertight container, and fill the space around the roots with the special aggregate. Although the potting soil can be left on the roots using the system illustrated, with other methods you should wash all the soil off the roots first, then repot in a special planting basket containing an aggregate such as expanded clay granules to anchor the roots.

2 With hydroponics the roots grow in water, but the level must not drop too low or be too deep. You must use a water-level indicator so that you know when more water is needed. Some systems use a visible float that tells you what the water level is, others change colour when a top-up is required.

3 The water in the reservoir is usually sufficient to last weeks or even a month in cold weather without having to be topped up. With most systems you will need to use tap-water, not rain-water, as the special fertilizer works by reacting with impurities in the tap-water.

MAKING CONVERSIONS

The exact method of preparing a plant for hydroponic culture depends on the system you are using. You will usually have to wash off all the potting soil, so it is easier to start with a small plant than to convert a large one. Many different kinds of plants can be grown hydroponically, including cacti. The kit instructions will usually suggest good plants to start with, but it is always worth experimenting with others. You can sometimes buy plants already growing hydroponically.

First Aid for Plants

Don't panic if disaster appears to strike – if your plant collapses or begins to look very sick, you may be able to save it by taking prompt action.

1 If you notice insect pests on a plant you can use a spray, but indoors an insecticidal plant pin is easier and more convenient to use.

2 Some plants wilt if they need misting to provide humid air around their leaves, others may just appear to lack lustre or begin to go brown at the edges. Misting will also help to control some types of pests that do not like a humid atmosphere.

3 If the potting soil has become very dry with a hard surface, much of the water you add will probably just run down the sides of the pot instead of penetrating the root-ball. Loosening the surface with a fork will help a dried-out root-ball to absorb water.

4 If the potting soil is saturated, perhaps with water standing in the saucer or cache pot, you need to draw excess moisture from the root-ball as quickly as possible. Knock the plant out of its pot and wrap the root-ball in absorbent paper – kitchen paper is good provided you use enough layers, or you can use newspaper.

5 Change the paper as soon as it is saturated. Leave the plant out of its pot, in a warm but not very hot position, until the compost is almost dry. Return the plant to its original pot, and be careful not to overwater in future. If the roots have been waterlogged for too long, they may have started to rot, or diseases may have entered. If the plant shows no signs of recovery after a couple of days, discard it.

DIGGING DEEPER

A plant sometimes collapses because the roots have been attacked by pests or diseases. If the potting soil does not appear to be excessively dry or wet, check the roots – removing some of the soil if necessary. If the roots are black and soft, discard the plant and do not use the old potting soil for other plants. If you find pests – particularly maggot-like grubs – kill them, wash the old potting soil off the roots, and repot in fresh, sterilized potting soil.

Some for Shade

Plants that tolerate low light levels are especially useful houseplants. They can be positioned by shady windows and within any room, perhaps on a table or sideboard, and still survive for a reasonable time. You can use any plant in these conditions, but after a while most will become sickly and deteriorate to a point at which they are no longer attractive. The plants listed here are only a selection of those suitable for a low-light position, but they are tough and dependable.

PLANTS TO TRY
Aglaonema
Anthurium
Asplenium nidus
Billbergia
Calathea
Cissus rhombifolia
Dieffenbachia
Dracaena
Fatsia
Ficus pumila
Hedera helix
Howea
Maranta
Monstera
Philodendron
Platycerium
Sansevieria
Spathiphyllum
Syngonium

Plants that can be used within the room because they tolerate lower light levels are especially useful. The basket on the left contains a spathiphyllum and trailing *Ficus pumila*. The pot on the right holds *Cissus rhombifolia* 'Ellen Danica'.

Sunshine Plants

It's usually difficult to give houseplants enough light for really healthy and even growth, yet ironically a position on a windowsill in full sun will probably injure or kill most of them! Sun through unshaded glass is much more intense than sun in the open – it acts like a magnifying glass and will often scorch vulnerable foliage. Although most plants will benefit from early and late sun, when the intensity is not too great, you need really tough sun-lovers to tolerate the hot midday sun intensified though glass. Most cacti and succulents are ideal, but try some of the other plants suggested here to create variety. Some that benefit from winter sun may be harmed in summer sun.

SOME LIKE IT HOT

Most cacti and succulents are naturally adapted to hot and dry conditions, where the sun beats down on them relentlessly. For this reason desert cacti make excellent windowsill plants. You will find popular cacti such as echinocactus, ferocactus, opuntias, parodias, and rebutias readily available at garden centres. If you don't care for cacti, try some of the other sun-loving succulents such as ceropegias, lithops, and kalanchoës. You will find a greater variation in shape and growth habit among the succulents, and there are lots to choose from.

Most houseplants prefer some sunlight but not strong, intense sun through glass. Use tough plants like hosta (left) and *Beaucarnea recurvata* (right) in the front line provided the position is not too hot, with plants that benefit from more shade behind, such as this cycas.

Pelargonium, Regal

Zebrina pendula

Cyperus diffusus

Impatiens, New
Guinea type

Gardenia jasminoides

Yucca

Cacti

Kalanchoë

Chlorophytum

Anthurium
scherzerianum

Codiaeum

Plectranthus coleoides 'Marginatus'

Tradescantia fluminensis 'Variegata'

PLANTS TO TRY

Ananas
Coleus
Hippeastrum (amaryllis)
Hoya carnosa
Kalanchoë blossfeldiana
Pachystachys
Pelargonium
Plectranthus fruticosus
Punica granatum var. nana
Roses (miniature)
Sansevieria trifasciata
 'Laurentii'
Yucca

Look at page 55

Imaginative Containers

A distinctive container can make a mediocre plant look good. Choosing an appropriate container is just as important as choosing the right plant, and can be just as much fun.

Garden centres and other shops sell a wonderful array of containers of all kinds, so lack of choice is no excuse. Some are expensive, but others are amazingly cheap if you shop around. You can also pick up some interesting containers from jumble sales or rummage sales. Some of the most imaginative containers may cost you nothing. An old soup bowl or old-fashioned brown cooking pot will make an interesting container, but will be especially appropriate in the kitchen. Galvanized buckets, old wicker baskets, a garden trug, an old terrine that you no longer use for its intended purpose, can all be given a new lease of life as decorative plant holders.

Drinking beakers, even painted jam-jars, can be pressed into use. Be careful not to use kitchen utensils for the sake of it, however, as there is sometimes a fine line between looking good and lapsing into bad taste. Patio pots and wall pots intended to go outdoors can be used very successfully indoors too. Some terracotta pots and wall pots are very ornate. Baskets of all kinds make good short-term plant holders, but you'll need to line them with a sheet of plastic to retain the potting soil and reduce the risk of water running through on to your furniture.

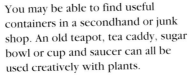

You may be able to find useful containers in a secondhand or junk shop. An old teapot, tea caddy, sugar bowl or cup and saucer can all be used creatively with plants.

THE BOTTOM LINE

The trouble with improvised containers is that usually they either have no drainage holes or are so open they can barely hold the potting soil. Very few houseplants will tolerate waterlogged conditions (cyperus and acorus are examples of those that will grow in standing water), so water must be able to drain away. Either make some holes and stand the container on a drip tray or keep the plant in an ordinary pot and use the decorative container as a cache pot.

If you do this, use a pot a size or two smaller than the outer pot, and add a layer of gravel or charcoal to raise the inner pot off the base. There must be enough space for surplus drainage water to stand without being in contact with the inner pot. To improve the visual appearance, you may prefer to pack more potting soil in the gap between the sides – even bringing it over the rim of the inner pot. The drawback to this is that it's difficult to lift the inner pot to ensure that the base isn't standing in water.

An old galvanized watering-can would look great in the conservatory or porch, while earthenware and stoneware containers are ideal for kitchen plants.

Anything with copper or brass in it fits in really well in an old cottage or wherever you want to enhance a period atmosphere with your houseplants.

Showing off with Foliage

Foliage plants will probably form the backbone of your indoor plant arrangements, and with care they will last in good condition for months and perhaps years. For instant effect, be prepared to buy large specimens – one really impressive plant will probably have more impact than three smaller ones, at the same total cost.

You will get more impact from small foliage plants if you group them together as part of a mixed arrangement instead of displaying them as individual specimens in their own pots.

1 No matter how striking the room setting, it will usually benefit from a few plants. This room is very stylish, but it looks harsh and rather bare.

2 If the room is large, you will need good-sized plants to make much impact. This weeping fig (*Ficus benjamina*) is bold enough to transform the room instantly.

3 Use trailers to clothe bare expanses of wall. Good use has been made of the ledge to accommodate a spider plant (*Chlorophytum comosum* 'Vittatum') and a *Mikania ternata*. The *Ficus pumila* on top of the stove softens the harsh angles. Obviously the plants would have to be moved away from the stove when it is in use. In a high-ceilinged room, use tall, vertical plants to break up a bare wall.

4 Adding plants will often improve the immediate area but can emphasize bare areas in the immediate vicinity. Be prepared to add more plants to fill in gaps, and bear in mind that a table can usually be improved with a small plant to act as a focal point.

5 Use foliage plants to create a framework, as these will be long-lasting and should not require frequent replacement. But use one or two flowering ones if you want to add a dash of colour. A bowl of fruit can play a similar role.

Showing off with Flowers

Most flowering houseplants bloom for weeks rather than months, and they may be at their peak for only a matter of days. Make the most of that short time by placing them where they can really show off. If you have a limited budget, you'll get greater pleasure from buying one fresh flowering plant that is just coming into bloom every week or two than by splashing out on a dozen at once but then going without blooms because you have a house full of plants that have all finished flowering.

1 Foliage plants can go on looking good for months or even years, but no matter how much you move them around they will become predictable and perhaps boring. Adding a more transient flowering plant can make all the difference to the display.

2 When the flowering plant is just beginning to bloom, and once it has passed its peak but while it remains colourful, tuck it in amongst other plants to give a suggestion of colour without putting it in the spotlight.

Be prepared to move the group around, perhaps to a light but not too sunny windowsill. The effect will be different and the plants will probably benefit from more natural light for a period.

3 While the plant is at its peak, bring it to the fore and make it the focal point, with the foliage plants providing an attractive backdrop.

DECORATIVE HOUSEPLANTS

Over the Edge

Use trailing plants imaginatively, to add colour or interest to an otherwise uninspiring shelf, or to cascade gracefully from a wall pot, forming a focal point on the wall like a picture.

MATERIALS AND TOOLS
Indoor hanging pot or "basket" with
    in-built drip tray or reservoir
Lightweight potting soil
Selection of 3–4 trailing plants

indoor hanging pot

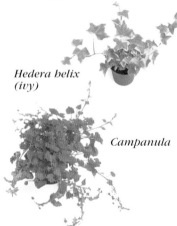

Hedera helix (ivy)

Campanula

WATERING WISDOM

Watering a hanging container or a wall pot is difficult. Simply having to reach above head height means you can't easily see where the water is going, and unless you apply it very sparingly there will be drips.

The solution is simple. Take the pot down for watering. If it contains long, trailing plants that make it difficult to place on a flat surface without causing damage, make yourself a pedestal to stand it on.

1 Fill the container with lightweight potting soil.

2 Plant some trailing foliage plants such as ivies around the edge, spacing them evenly.

3 Plant a trailing flowering plant, such as a cascading campanula, to flow over the edge. Leave space for a centrepiece plant – in this case a low-growing upright campanula.

4 Fill any gaps with more potting soil, and firm in well. Water carefully.

Pedestal Perfection

Plant up a pot with trailing plants and place it on a pedestal. The results will be stunning. Watering is easier than with a hanging container, and because the light is often better at this height than close to the ceiling, your plants will probably be healthier too. You'll also find it easier to keep an eye on the plants and to shape and groom them to produce a curtain of cascading growth around the pedestal.

MATERIALS AND TOOLS
Shallow bowl or dish with drainage
    hole
Crocks or chipped bark
Potting soil
Selection of trailing plants

shallow bowl

*Mikania ternata
(syn. M. dentata)*

*Sedum sieboldii
'Mediovariegatum'*

Columnea

1 Cover the drainage hole with crocks or chipped bark, then half-fill the container with potting soil.

2 While still in their pots, arrange the plants the way you want them.

3 Plant some foliage trailers at the front first – these will take over as the showy plants once the flowering plant behind has finished blooming.

4 Including a flowering trailer will add interest and colour, but try to avoid having only flowering plants, otherwise the period of interest may be limited.

Hide and Seek

Most of us grow houseplants simply because we find them attractive in their own right, but you can also use them to mask an unattractive feature. That way you get double value – you replace the visually unattractive with something beautiful.

1 We have to put up with radiators to benefit from their warmth, but it's useful to be able to hide some of the associated plumbing.

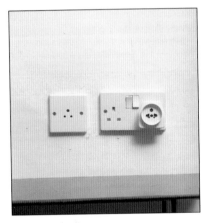

1 Useful and essential as wall sockets are, they can spoil the look of a room. You may be able to place a small table in front of them and position a suitable plant to hide them.

2 This *Begonia rex* is ideal as its large leaves hide the wall behind, yet the plant is not so sprawling or leafy that it is difficult to use the sockets.

1 Ventilator grilles also look unattractive, but they are easy to conceal with a group of plants.

2 Try placing an attractive mixed group like this in front of it – a plain wall behind can create a stunning effect. Don't place plants in front of the grille of a warm-air duct that's in use.

2 Try masking it with a tall plant, but choose a tough one, like this ficus, if the radiator is in use. In general, use plants to conceal radiators in the summer, when they are not in use, as most plants will not tolerate standing by a hot radiator.

Going up the Pole

In the wild, species that are popular as houseplants, such as *Epipremnum aureum*, monsteras and philodendrons, scramble up and through trees. They have developed aerial roots by which they cling and gain moisture and nutrients. Give them a helping hand by providing a moss-covered pole. You can buy one or make your own.

MATERIALS AND TOOLS
Large pot
Crocks or chipped bark
Moss-covered pole
Large stones or pebbles
Potting soil
Scrambling plant with aerial roots
Plastic-covered wire

pot

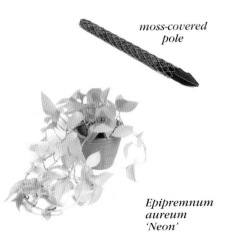

moss-covered pole

Epipremnum aureum 'Neon'

1 Cover the drainage hole with crocks or chipped bark, then position the moss pole. Use large stones or pebbles to anchor it in position.

2 Almost fill the pot with potting soil, firming it around the pole and between the stones.

3 Plant your trailing or climbing plant. Choose one that will soon cover the pole but will not grow too large.

4 The plant may eventually support itself, but initially you will have to tie or wire the stems into position on the pole.

Climbing High

Climbers are some of the most difficult plants to display successfully in the home. If left untrained they usually grow too tall, with lots of foliage towards the ceiling but bare towards the base. The knack is to use an appropriate support and to prune and train as often as necessary to maintain an attractive shape.

MATERIALS AND TOOLS
Large heavy pot
Crocks or chipped bark
Potting soil
Climbing plant frame
Climbing plant

Ficus pumila

pot

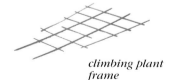

climbing plant frame

1 Cover the drainage hole with crocks or chipped bark, then part-fill the pot with potting soil while holding the frame in position.

2 Plant in front of the frame and top up with more potting soil. Firm in well and then water. This plant is a trailer rather than a climber, so allow some stems to trail over the edge of the pot and train others to climb through the frame.

3 For a more vigorous climber like *Cissus rhombifolia* 'Ellen Danica' you will need a larger pot, and all the stems should be trained to the frame.

Palm Court

Palms look graceful and elegant. They usually look best in isolation or among other palms, rather than in a group of mixed plants. Display them so that their classic shape can be appreciated. Allow these "aristocrats" space to make a statement.

MATERIALS AND TOOLS
Decorative pot with drainage hole
Crocks or chipped bark
Potting soil (loam-based if the
    plant is large)
Palm, appropriate for size of pot

palm

decorative pot

crocks

DISPLAYING PALMS

Palms can look splendid in isolation, but they usually look more impressive if you have a collection of them. But don't crowd them. Display plants of different sizes to add interest, and perhaps place small ones on pedestals in front of taller ones in large pots.

1 Unless your palm is small (a few never grow large in the home), choose a large pot. As it will be conspicuous, choose an attractive, decorative one that does the plant justice. Start by placing a layer of crocks or other drainage material in the bottom.

2 Part-fill the container with potting soil. If the plant is large use a soil-based mixture as this will give greater stability if it grows tall, and also the plant is less likely to run out of nutrients.

3 Water the plant thoroughly and allow the surplus water to drain, then knock the palm out of its original pot. Tease out a few roots to encourage it to root quickly into the new potting soil.

4 Place the root-ball in the pot to check planting depth. Add or remove potting soil until the top of the root-ball is about 2.5 cm (1 in) below the rim (less if the pot is small). Finish potting by trickling more potting soil into the gap between the root-ball and pot, firming it well. Press it down with your fingers or use a piece of wood to remove any pockets of air.

Staggering Ferns

The stag's-horn fern (*Platycerium bifurcatum*) is usually sold growing in pots, but you can make it into a stunning talking-point by mounting it on bark and hanging it on a wall as living "antlers".

MATERIALS AND TOOLS
Piece of cork bark
Sharp knife or chisel
Pointed tool or drill
Plastic-covered wire
Sphagnum moss
Platycerium bifurcatum

Platycerium bifurcatum

Sphagnum moss

1 Prepare the bark by using a sharp knife or chisel to flatten the area where you want to place the fern. By doing this you will ensure that you can fix the fern in position firmly.

2 Make some fine holes through the bark with a sharp tool or a drill, so that you can pass a length of wire through them on either side of your fern.

3 Place a handful of the sphagnum moss against the flattened area where you intend to fix the fern.

4 Knock the plant out of its pot and remove some of the root-ball if it's too large. Wrap the root-ball in sphagnum moss, then position it on the bark.

Make an Epiphyte Tree

Not all plants have to be displayed in pots. Those that naturally grow on trees (epiphytes) – mostly bromeliads and orchids – can be arranged on an old branch, and will look much more exotic displayed like this.

MATERIALS AND TOOLS
Large, heavy pot
Rocks or stones
Branches from an old tree
Quick-setting plaster
Selection of small epiphytic plants
Sphagnum moss
Plastic-covered wire

epiphytic plants

plaster

rocks

1 First, place enough rocks in the pot to stabilize the branches, but make sure that you leave enough space to insert the branches. Angle the branches for maximum stability – it is vital to make sure that you do not place the centre of gravity to one side of the pot – then surround with plaster. It will help if you get someone else to hold the branches in position while you firm the plaster around the branches and rocks.

2 Once the plaster has set you can "plant" your epiphytes. Remove each plant from its pot. If it has a small root system you may be able to remove a lot of the potting soil to reduce the size of the root-ball. The smaller the root-ball, the easier it will be to site it on the branch. Wrap the reduced root-ball in the moss.

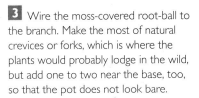

3 Wire the moss-covered root-ball to the branch. Make the most of natural crevices or forks, which is where the plants would probably lodge in the wild, but add one to two near the base, too, so that the pot does not look bare.

4 When you are satisfied with your arrangement, use green plastic-coated wire to secure the plants in position. Mist all the leaves and root-balls thoroughly.

Amazing Air Plants

Plants that live off air and require no soil, not even moss around their roots, sound incredible – but that's exactly what the tillandsia group of air plants can do. They have evolved so that they can absorb moisture and nutrients from the air. That means these surprisingly tough plants can be used around the home almost like ornaments. Fix them to pieces of driftwood or bark, or use specially formulated glue to attach them to mirrors, shells and ornaments. You could even keep a collection of air plants laid loose in a small basket.

MATERIALS AND TOOLS
Driftwood
Air plants
Silicone adhesive
Decorative shells

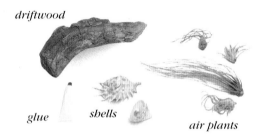

driftwood

glue   *shells*

air plants

1 Experiment with the position of the plants until you are pleased with the effect. Don't glue them until the arrangement looks right.

2 You don't need much adhesive, just enough to secure the plant in position. Follow the manufacturer's instructions.

3 Fix each plant in turn, making sure it looks right. Hold the plant just above the surface for a moment to make sure the best profile faces forward, then press it into position without crushing the leaves.

4 Air plants also look good in shells, and you may not even have to glue them into position if the shell has a suitable shape.

Make a Cactus Garden

Cactus gardens are really easy to look after, and they are a great way to grow cacti if you find isolated plants a little too boring. Creating a mixed bowl of them gives you plenty of scope to be creative, and every cactus garden will be unique.

MATERIALS AND TOOLS
Shallow bowl with drainage hole
Crocks or chipped bark
Cactus potting soil
Cacti
Newspaper
Fine gravel or stone chippings

shallow bowl

cacti

crocks

gravel

HOUSEPLANTS TIPS

• Water after planting, but water sparingly afterwards. In the winter most cacti will require water only occasionally – just enough to prevent them shrivelling.
• Most cacti should be kept cool (but frost-free) in winter. They are more likely to flower well after a cool spell.
• Always keep cacti in good light. They will tolerate full sun.

1 First, place crocks or chipped bark over the drainage hole, otherwise the potting soil will just be washed away when you water.

2 Make a bed of cactus soil. You can use an ordinary potting soil if you have no choice, but one designed for cacti will probably have extra grit and be very free-draining.

3 Plant the cacti at the same depth as they were in their original pots. As most cacti are very prickly and difficult to handle, make a gripper out of folded newspaper. This simple technique is very effective.

4 Finish off by covering the soil with a surface dressing of grit or small pebbles. This will greatly enhance the appearance of the finished garden.

Exotic Orchids

Orchids can make beautiful and exotic houseplants, but be warned, they can look very boring out of bloom. It is a good idea to grow them on in a greenhouse or conservatory – or even a spare room – for most of the year, and make a decorative arrangement out of them when they come into flower.

MATERIALS AND TOOLS
Basket
Plastic sheet
Fine gravel
Moss
3 orchids

Miltonia

Phalaenopsis

Paphiopedilum

basket

moss

1 Line the base of the basket with plastic, if it is not waterproof, bringing it just high enough up the sides to retain the gravel. Add a layer of gravel to help provide a humid atmosphere and to raise the pots to an appropriate height.

2 Line the sides of the basket with moss.

3 Arrange the orchids in the basket. Keep them in their pots to avoid disturbing their roots. This also means that you can replace a pot if the flowers die while the others are still in bloom.

4 Use more moss to hide the pots. If you keep it moist, it should go on looking good for as long as the orchids remain in bloom.

HOUSEPLANTS TIP

If the orchids need support, plant three or four canes around the edge of the arrangement and tie raffia around the outside to prevent the plants from drooping.

Mysterious Meat-eaters

There are many strange and interesting houseplants to be discovered. Carnivorous plants that naturally live in bogs may not look spectacular, but they make up for that with their fascinating lifestyle! Because bogs are usually low in nutrients, these plants have evolved to catch flies and other insects.

MATERIALS AND TOOLS
Small aquarium
Fine gravel
Charcoal
Potting soil
Carnivorous bog plants
Moss

small aquarium

Pinguicula

Drosera binata

Dionaea muscipula

gravel   *charcoal*

1 Place a layer of gravel in the bottom of the aquarium to allow surplus water to drain away.

2 Add a layer of charcoal, which will help to prevent any standing water from becoming smelly.

3 Add a layer of peat (peat moss) potting soil. Use only sufficient to accommodate the root-balls – leave plenty of space above for the stems to benefit from the protected environment created by the glass.

4 Scoop out a hole for each plant, insert the root-ball, then firm in gently.

5 Arrange the plants so that they look as though they are growing in their natural environment. Don't overcrowd the aquarium.

6 Cover the surface with moss for an authentic bog look. Keep the moss and potting soil moist.

Christmas Cheer

The first bowl of hyacinths to bloom each year makes winter seem a little shorter and spring that tiny bit nearer. And if you use prepared (treated) bulbs you can have them in flower a month or so before the normal ones. Use the same technique for planting and growing both kinds, but plant prepared bulbs as soon as possible after they come on sale. The special treatment makes them think the year is more advanced than it is.

MATERIALS AND TOOLS
Bowl or pot
Pebbles or crocks for drainage
Potting soil or bulb fibre
Prepared (treated) hyacinth bulbs
Newspaper

bowl or pot

hyacinth bulb

pebbles

newspaper

1 If using a container with a drainage hole, cover the hole with a few pebbles or pieces of broken pot. If these are not available, use large pieces of chipped bark. If you use a bowl without drainage holes, use a special bulb fibre intended for the purpose. Part-fill the container with the potting soil or bulb fibre (if using bulb fibre for a solid container, make sure it is moist but not soggy).

FINISHING TOUCHES

You can make your bowl of hyacinths look even prettier by growing grass or placing moss between the bulbs. Sow grass seed as soon as the bulbs are brought indoors. Cut it with scissors if it grows too long. Moss can be added at the last minute.

2 If you are planting a single bulb, place it in the centre; for larger bowls use three or five bulbs (an odd number looks better). Top up with more potting soil or bulb fibre, but leave just the noses of the bulbs exposed.

3 Cover with newspaper to keep out the light, then put in a cool place. The best place may be in the garden, covered with sand or peat. If you do this, keep the newspaper on top to keep the bulbs and bowl clean.

Flowering Dry

Bulbs that flower on a windowsill without being planted are also fun, and another entertaining project for children. You can be almost sure of a flower, probably within weeks. But be warned ... *Sauromatum venosum*, the voodoo lily, looks amazing, but it smells putrid when the flower opens fully. For children this can be part of the fun, of course.

MATERIALS AND TOOLS
Sauromatum venosum
   (voodoo lily) tubers
saucer or small dish
fine gravel, stone chippings or sand

voodoo lily tuber

gravel

flat dish

1 Buy sauromatum tubers in spring. You can simply stand them in a light place and watch them grow, but it's best to use a bed of sand, grit or fine gravel to keep them upright. Use a shallow saucer or similar small container.

NOT THE END

The smell will disappear as suddenly as it arrived. You can then leave the lily to produce its large, hand-shaped leaves – a feature in their own right. But the plant will soon become top-heavy and have to be discarded. Alternatively, you can plant the tubers in the garden where you can enjoy their bold foliage display during the summer.

2 Push the base of the bulb gently into the sand or grit, with the nose as near vertical as possible. This is just to keep the plant stable.

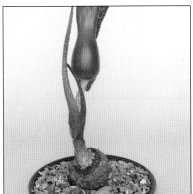

3 Do not water – the flowering stem grows rapidly even though the bulb has not been planted.

Beautiful Baskets

A basket is a great way to display a small group of houseplants. You don't need a lot of plants to make a super show, and when one goes past its best you can just remove it and pop in another plant.

MATERIALS AND TOOLS
Basket
Plastic sheet
Potting soil
5–6 small plants
Reindeer moss or fresh moss

basket

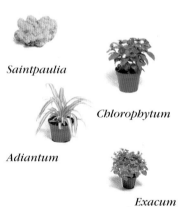

Saintpaulia

Chlorophytum

Adiantum

Exacum

1 To protect the basket (and your furniture) from the effects of moisture, line it with a piece of plastic cut to size.

2 Add a layer of potting soil to retain moisture and provide a humid atmosphere around the plants.

3 Remove the plants from their pots and place in the basket. It may be necessary to remove some potting soil from the bottom or add a little more to bring each plant to the right height.

4 Make sure you are entirely happy with the arrangement, then trickle a little more potting soil between the plants to fill in the gaps.

5 Use dried or fresh moss to fill any visible spaces between the plants.

HOUSEPLANTS TIP
You could leave the plants in the individual pots for convenience.

Summer Blooming "Bulbs"

Most of us pot up a few bulbs or corms for winter colour, but summer-flowering bulbs, corms and tubers tend to get neglected. This is a pity because there are some wonderful flowers to be enjoyed. Begonias and gloxinias are just as easy to grow as winter bulbs; plant them in the spring.

MATERIALS AND TOOLS
Begonia or gloxinia tuber
2 small pots
Peat-based potting soil

pots

*begonia or
gloxinia tuber*

WHICH WAY UP?

If small shoots are forming, you will know which way up to plant. If not, follow this advice: a begonia tuber has a slight hollow on the top, so plant with this upward; gloxinias (grown the same way as tuberous begonias) are more rounded on top, and the remains of old roots may still be around the base.

1 For a begonia tuber, fill the pot almost to the top with potting soil.

2 Firm down gently with the base of another pot.

3 Press the base of the tuber into good contact with the potting soil, but leave the top exposed.

4 You will get larger flowers if you remove the two smaller female flowers (these usually have "wings" behind them) that you find either side of the male flower in the centre. Just pinch them out as soon as you notice them.

5 Plant gloxinia tubers in the same way as tuberous begonias, but plant with the hairy side downwards (the hairs are the remains of old roots). Instead of planting into a small pot first, you may prefer to start them off in their final 13–15 cm (5–6 in) pots.

Indoor Topiary

Proper topiary is not practical indoors, but you can cheat a little and achieve a similar effect by training ivy over a frame. Start with an easy shape like the lollipop shown here, but once you are proficient you can experiment with all kinds of imaginative shapes. Buy a wire frame or make your own.

MATERIALS AND TOOLS
Wire frame
Pot large enough to accommodate
 frame
Crocks or chipped bark
Potting soil
2–3 small-leaved ivies

wire frame

pot

variegated small-leaved ivy

2 Place a layer of potting soil in the base. Do not make this too deep, as the base of the frame should be low down in the pot for stability.

3 Insert the wire frame, making sure it is placed centrally.

1 Place crocks or large pieces of chipped bark over the drainage hole in the base of the pot.

4 Add potting soil to secure the frame, but don't fill the pot completely yet.

5 Insert the ivies around the edge of the pot. The more plants that you use, the more quickly the frame will be covered – two or three is about right.

6 Leave a few shoots to trail over the edge of the pot, but thread the rest through the frame. Within a few months the frame will probably be completely hidden by the new growth. Thread new shoots through bare areas, and pinch back any that are too long. Regular pinching back of long shoots will help to retain the shape once the frame has been covered.

Beautiful Bonsai

Bonsai (dwarfed trees) can look even more beautiful when grown as a group, and a forest group can be particularly pleasing to create. If this is the first time you have ever attempted to grow bonsai, it is probably best to use relatively cheap trees so that you will not have made an expensive mistake if things don't quite work out the way you planned them. Use an odd number of trees because this creates a more balanced and natural appearance – five is the minimum for a group like this.

MATERIALS AND TOOLS
Trees (bonsai)
Container
Branch cutters (pruning shears)
Wire mesh or crocks
Potting soil
Moss or fine stone chippings
  (optional)

container

*branch cutters
(pruning shears)*

1 Select a tree to dominate the group and position this first. Prepare it by removing some of the lower branches with branch cutters or pruning shears.

2 Place wire mesh or crocks over the drainage holes, then part-fill the container with potting soil. Plant your dominant tree. You may find that you have to remove some of the old potting soil from the root-ball, and shorten some of the roots.

3 Place the second-largest tree just to the right of the first one. Adjust it until it looks right – again, you may have to trim some of the branches and roots.

4 Position the third tree close to the second, again to the right. Avoid planting in a straight line, so that the group looks natural when viewed from the side.

5 Position the smaller remaining trees to the left of the group. This is how they might grow at the edge of a forest.

BONSAI TIPS

• Although a mixed group can be effective, it's better to stick to trees of the same kind. This makes it easier to create a natural-looking scene.

• When viewed from the front, try to make sure that no three trees are in a straight line, and that the trunk of one is not hidden by another in front of it.

• It is best to use a shallow oval or rectangular container.

• If the dish is shallow and the trees relatively tall, you may wish to wire the root-balls into position. Use copper or other easily bent wire, threaded through the mesh covering the drainage holes, and then around the root-ball. Once the container has been topped up with potting soil, you won't see the wires.

6 Trim back any long shoots that are making the group look unbalanced. Top off with more potting soil, and, if desired, finish off with a layer of moss or fine stone chippings.

Mixed Blessings

A bowl of mixed plants almost always looks better than the same number dotted around in individual pots. Garden centres and florists often sell mixed bowls, but you can probably make one more cheaply using a container that you already have ... and you can ring the changes with different plants.

MATERIALS AND TOOLS
Bowl with drainage hole
Crocks or chipped bark
Potting soil
Collection of mixed foliage and
    flowering plants
Spare pot the same size as
    centrepiece plant pot

bowl

foliage and flowering plants

1 Cover the drainage hole with a piece of broken pot or chipped bark to allow all surplus moisture to drain while holding back the potting soil.

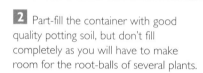

2 Part-fill the container with good quality potting soil, but don't fill completely as you will have to make room for the root-balls of several plants.

3 It's a good idea to have a centrepiece plant – either a taller foliage plant or a smaller flowering plant to contrast with mainly foliage plants. Insert an empty pot temporarily so that you are sure of leaving enough space for your centrepiece.

4 Place the other plants around the main focal-point plant, rearranging them as necessary while still in their pots. Do not start planting until you are happy with the results.

5 Finally, insert the central plant. If it is likely to be a long-term occupant, remove it from its pot like the others. If you are likely to have to replace it after a few weeks – as is common with flowering plants once they finish blooming – keep it in its pot. Changing the colour of the flowering plant means you can mix and match the arrangement to suit various situations in the house. Here you can see how two plants can enhance very different positions.

Waste-not Brighteners

Don't discard summer bedding plants that you have no space for in the garden. Why not pot them up for an indoor display? Many compact bedding plants can be used, such as ageratum and French (dwarf) marigolds. Fibrous-rooted begonias and Busy Lizzies (impatiens) can be especially good. Do remember to feed them. They will gradually deteriorate indoors but they should give you many weeks of pleasure before they are past their best.

MATERIALS AND TOOLS
Decorative pot
Crocks or chipped bark
Potting soil
Bedding plants

1 Place some crocks or chipped bark over the drainage hole in the pot, then a layer of potting soil.

French (dwarf) marigolds

decorative pot

2 Remove the spare bedding plants from their container carefully and tease them apart so that the roots are disturbed as little as possible.

3 Here, a number of plants have been placed in one pot for an instant effect, but if you are prepared to wait you could use a single plant. It will fill a pot of this size within a few weeks.

4 Firm more potting soil between the plants to remove any large air pockets, then water thoroughly and allow to drain. Keep moist but not waterlogged, and feed regularly.

Pot up a Plant

Another money-saving idea for short-term houseplants is to dig up a few plants from your garden. You will probably have to return them to the garden, because they will begin to deteriorate or become too large, but you can enjoy some impressive plants indoors for next to nothing.

MATERIALS AND TOOLS
Garden plant
Trowel or spade
Large pot
Potting soil
Gravel (optional)

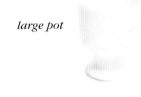

large pot

trowel or spade

1 Choose a small plant that will fit into a pot, or take a piece from the edge of a larger one. Lift it with plenty of soil around the roots. Test for size; you may need to remove more soil or choose a larger container.

2 Add a layer of potting soil deep enough to bring the plant to the right height. A container like this may not have a drainage hole, but provided you do not plan to keep the plant indoors for many weeks it may not matter. Place some drainage material such as gravel in the bottom just to be sure that there is no chance of waterlogging.

3 Position the plant in the top and firm in with some more potting soil.

4 Water in, but be careful not to over-water if there aren't any drainage holes in the container.

Stupid cunt

Dish up a Display

You can make a group of ordinary houseplants look something special by grouping them together in a decorative bowl. You don't even have to worry about eventual sizes and growth rates if you are prepared to split the group and grow them on individually after a few months.

MATERIALS AND TOOLS
Decorative bowl
Crocks or chipped bark
Fine gravel
Potting soil
3–5 foliage and flowering plants

decorative bowl

fine gravel

Kalanchoë

Dracaena sanderiana

Ficus pumila

Pteris

1 Cover the drainage hole, if there is one, with crocks or large pieces of chipped bark. If there isn't one, you will have to water very carefully to avoid waterlogging. Place a layer of fine gravel in the base.

2 Part-fill with potting soil – the amount to add will depend on the size of the container and the depth of the root-balls.

3 Position a trailing plant so that it cascades over the edge. This will make the group look more interesting.

4 Try to include a flowering plant. If this is impossible, include one with bright and colourful foliage.

Start a Collection

Once houseplants become more of a consuming hobby than just a passing pleasure, you will soon begin to look for more ways to feed your passion. One of the best ways is to start a collection of a particular type of plants, whether it's a large and very diverse group such as cacti, or a smaller but interesting group like saintpaulias (African violets).

MATERIALS AND TOOLS
Collection of plants
Baskets or containers of various sizes
Florist's foam
Knife
Moss

baskets

florist's foam

moss

*saintpaulias
(African violets)*

1 Start by grouping your plants in their likely final positions – but be prepared to keep changing them until they look right.

2 The design will look more interesting if you can create a cascade effect. Raise the pots in the middle row so that they are halfway between the back and the front plants.

3 Build up the back of the display using florist's foam. Cut it to size and place it beneath small baskets to raise them to a suitable height.

4 Arrange the plants at the back, then fill in the space in front in steps. Try the plants for size so that you can use more foam beneath the pots if needed.

HOUSEPLANTS TIP

The more you collect, the more imaginatively you will want to display your plants. Just one idea is shown here, but the possibilities are endless.

5 Arrange the plants so that they look as though they could be growing as a natural group, rather than planting them in a straight row. Finish off the arrangement by filling the spaces between the pots with moss.

Bottle it Up

Bottle gardens are great fun to make, and if you choose a stoppered bottle you will probably be able to grow some of those tricky plants that demand very high humidity. Don't worry too much about choosing the right plants, however. If you are prepared to replace plants when they outgrow their space, just concentrate on the plants that please you. You will have to improvise tools for your bottle garden by lashing old pieces of cutlery to garden canes (stakes).

MATERIALS AND TOOLS
Large glass bottle with cork
Paper or thin cardboard
Fine gravel
Charcoal
Potting soil
Knife, fork, spoon and cotton reel
(spool) attached to canes (stakes)
Small foliage plants

large glass bottle with cork

fine gravel   *charcoal*

small foliage plants

bottle gardening tools

1 Place some fine gravel in the bottom of the bottle. If the neck is narrow you can make yourself a funnel from paper or thin cardboard to scatter it evenly over the base.

2 Add a thin layer of charcoal. This will help to absorb impurities and reduce the risk of the bottle smelling if there is too much moisture.

3 Spread a layer of potting soil over the base, and level it. Using your improvised trowel, make a hole for the plant. In a wide-necked bottle you can scoop it out with your hand, but if the neck is narrow your spoon lashed to a piece of cane (stake) may be essential.

4 Firm the plant in well. If you can't reach with your hand, use a cotton reel (spool) pushed on to the end of a cane to tamp down the soil.

5 Work round the whole bottle until it is fully planted. Place a tall or very colourful plant in the centre if appropriate. Then mist the plants. Aim the spray at the sides of the bottle if potting soil is clinging to the glass and is spoiling the effect. Leave the plants and potting soil moist but not soaking wet.

HOUSEPLANT DISPLAYS

BALANCING THE BOTTLE

Place the cork firmly in position and leave it for a day or two. Some misting of the glass, especially in the morning, is quite normal – but if it never clears there is too much moisture, so leave the cork off for a day and try again. If no condensation appears at all, it is probably too dry – mist again, then return the cork. It will take trial and error at first, but once the bottle is balanced you can leave it for months without attention, although you will have to prune or remove plants that become too large.

6 If using a stoppered bottle you will have to balance the atmosphere over a week or two. You may have to keep inserting or removing the cork for periods (see above).

61

Terrariums are Terrific

Terrariums are similar to bottle gardens and come in a variety of shapes. Many of them are not sealed, so the atmosphere is less humid. They are generally a more ornamental way to display plants. If access is easy, you may want to consider a few flowering plants to provide colour.

MATERIALS AND TOOLS
Terrarium
Expanded clay granules
Gravel
Potting soil
Selection of small plants

terrarium

1 Place a layer of expanded clay granules, followed by gravel, in the base, to reduce the risk of the potting soil becoming waterlogged. Use either gravel or clay granules if you cannot get both.

2 Add the potting soil, making the layer several inches deep if possible. If this is not practical because of the design of the terrarium, you will need to reduce the depth of the root-balls.

3 If your centrepiece plant is too large, try just a little judicious pruning with scissors.

gravel   *expanded clay granules*

selection of small plants

4 You should be able to plant and firm the plants in by hand. Plant the back, or the least accessible area, first.

5 Fill in the gaps, if possible placing the plants most likely to require regular pruning or pinching back in the most accessible positions.

6 Plant your centrepiece plant, firming it in well.

A Pretty Pot-et-fleur

Make cut flowers go further and ring the changes with your foliage groups by making an attractive pot-et-fleur. Your basic group of plants will remain looking good for months to come, but you can change the cut flowers as often as necessary. You'll find that a few flowers go a long way with this kind of arrangement.

MATERIALS AND TOOLS
Basket or other decorative container
5 foliage plants
Vase
Plastic sheet
Cut flowers
Scissors

basket

vase

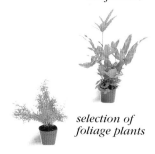

cut flowers

selection of foliage plants

1 Have a trial run by placing the plants and vase in the container first, moving them around as necessary until you have a pleasing arrangement.

4 Try to cover as much of the container as possible with foliage. There is no need to worry about packing the plants in tightly, as they will benefit from the microclimate created.

2 Having decided on how the plants and vase should be arranged, line the basket with a plastic sheet to protect it from moisture (this will not be necessary if you use a waterproof planter).

3 Position the vase before you start arranging the foliage plants. This is a large vase for the size of the potted plants, and you may prefer to use a smaller one that is easier to conceal. A small bunch of freesias can look as pretty as a group of taller flowers.

5 Try to keep the length of the cut-flower stems in proportion to the overall arrangement. Don't forget that cutting off the end of the stem may help the flower to take up water more easily, and a cut-flower preservative in the water will also help.

Great Gifts

Houseplants make ideal gifts for those friends and relatives for whom you find it difficult to choose a present – and of course they are perfect as housewarming presents or as a thank-you gift after a stay. But try to put a little thought into the kind of plant you choose.

You will probably find a wider range of plants at a garden centre than at a florist or flower shop. And whatever the season, you will always find flowering plants like year-round chrysanthemums and these begonias.

You will have to pay a bit more for a plant like an orchid – this is a miltonia – but it is sure to be appreciated. Remember that not everyone is knowledgeable about plants, so if the label or wrapper does not have cultural instructions, copy such information from a book on to a small card. It will show that you have given your gift a little extra thought.

Plants like lilies are usually sold in ordinary pots. You could make your gift more special by repotting into a decorative container that you know will go with the recipient's decor.

Right: Scented flowers like the stephanotis and freesias shown here are an especially appropriate gift for someone who has just moved into a new house, or for someone who you know loves perfumes.

Year-round chrysanthemums (above) and *Begonia elatior* hybrids (the ones you see on sale in flower all the year round - below) are a "safe" choice. They will bloom for weeks provided they are watered, and are usually discarded when flowering has finished.

If the recipient is horticulturally knowledgeable, a plant like an azalea is a good choice. With the right care these will flower for weeks and can go on to flower again in future years, but they can die within a week if not looked after.

Leave a Scent

Scented leaves have an advantage over fragrant flowers because you can enjoy their fragrance for a much longer period. You should be able to enjoy scented-leaved pelargoniums all year round. You can also group scented plants in close proximity without them competing with each other – scented-leaved plants usually release their fragrance only when you brush against them.

MATERIALS AND TOOLS
Large, decorative container
Crocks or chipped bark
Potting soil
Scented-leaved pelargoniums

Pelargonium 'Lady Plymouth'

Pelargonium 'Attar of Roses'

Pelargonium 'Royal Oak'

large, decorative container

Position a pelargonium near a wash basin where you will brush against it.

1 Use crocks to cover the drainage holes in the container.

2 Part-fill the container with a good potting soil.

3 Knock the plants out of their original pots and plant in the container. Some scented-leaved pelargoniums grow large, so leave sufficient space for growth or be prepared to pinch them back regularly.

4 Top up with more soil between the plants, and firm them in. You will already be appreciating the aromas as your hands brush the leaves!

All Change

Displaying houseplants is as much about choosing appropriate containers as it is about buying plants. An attractive and well-proportioned container can make a mediocre plant look good, while a really stunning plant can be disappointing if the pot is unsuitable. Try putting the same plant in a number of different containers – you will need no more convincing!

This container is an appropriate size and looks attractive without detracting from the plant itself.

You can keep the plant in its original growing pot and use different cache pots to decide on the most appropriate size and style. This pteris fern is clearly too large for a cache pot of this size. If you take it out of its growing pot and reduce the size of the root-ball, the proportions will still look wrong.

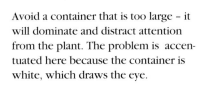

Avoid a container that is too large – it will dominate and distract attention from the plant. The problem is accentuated here because the container is white, which draws the eye.

Flowering plants have to be treated with particular sensitivity – you don't want to detract from the beauty of the blooms. Not only is this cache pot clearly too small, but the flowery design is also inappropriate.

This plain green pot is perfect – it looks tasteful in its own right and it also enhances the flowers.

Although this cache pot is the correct size, its design fights with the flowers instead of harmonizing with them. The choice of decoration and bright colour kills the impact of the pale flowers.

Ring the Changes

Usually you buy a plant and then look for an appropriate pot, but if you have some attractive containers you may want to find plants that will look good in them. You can create many different effects by choosing plants with different growth habits and shapes.

A mixture of mound-forming or trailing plants with upright ones tends to give equal prominence to plants and pots.

Plants with a cascading habit create a totally different effect, with the containers receding in importance. To make sure that the group doesn't lack a sense of height, you can raise one of the pots, as has been done here with the one at the back.

The effect of using tall, upright plants is to make more of a feature of the containers by leaving them exposed. According to how decorative the containers are, this can be a good or a bad thing.

Everything looks in proportion with this exacum, with its compact and rounded shape reflecting the shape and proportions of the pot.

The relationship of size and proportion between plant and pot can be crucial. Even if the root-ball of this fern had been reduced in size, the container would still look too small.

This cycas looks a trifle ridiculous. The wide base and low height of the container emphasizes the way these plants taper towards the base.

A Decorated Flowerpot

If you can't find a container that meets your needs or expresses your personality, why not paint a pot? You can create a design that looks really eye-catching, and as it will be unique it's bound to attract comment.

MATERIALS AND TOOLS
Paper
Pencil
Clay flowerpot
Acrylic paints
Fine and broad paintbrushes

clay flowerpot

paper and pencil

acrylic paints

fine and broad paintbrushes

HOUSEPLANTS TIP

In normal use your painted pot should remain looking bright for a long time, but eventually moisture seeping through the pot may take its toll. It's worth lining the inside of the pot with a piece of plastic before adding the potting soil, but be sure to make a drainage hole in the base.

1 Experiment with designs on paper first. You will be able to visualize the final result more easily, and if you are drawing freehand the practice will give you more confidence when you come to transfer the design to the pot.

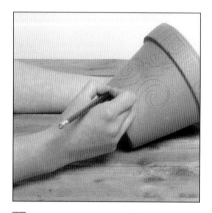

2 Draw the design on your pot in pencil – you can easily rub it out and redraw it if an unsteady hand lets you down first time around.

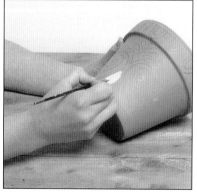

3 Apply the paint as evenly as possible, using steady strokes. Try to apply all of one colour before moving on to the next.

4 Complete one side of the pot and allow it to dry before turning to the next section. You can either cover the pot completely or plan a design that incorporates the natural terracotta.

Make and Mend

Improvising can be great fun, and if you do it successfully the results can be uniquely attractive. You can put your houseplants in all kinds of containers, but they often look best if household objects are used in appropriate settings – such as kitchen utensils for plants in the kitchen.

1 This old cake tin is a gentle pale green that harmonizes with the green ferns. You will almost certainly have similar, apparently unpromising items around the home – or in the garage or shed – that can be given a new lease of life with plants.

2 Teapots and kettles are a popular choice for the kitchen. You can use modern utensils, but something like this will have much more character. This *soleirolia (helxine)* will soon cascade right down the side.

3 Any bowl can be pressed into use. This spathiphyllum looks much more elegant in a bulbous container than it would in a more upright plant pot.

HOUSEPLANTS TIP

If you are using a container simply as a cachepot, you should have no problem with waterlogging provided the bottom of the pot is raised off the base and not allowed to stand in water. But if you are planting directly into the container it is advisable to make drainage holes in the base.

4 Plants always look good in copper or brass containers, especially in an old house. This impatiens looks really aristocratic in this happy marriage between plant and container.

5 The simple shape and muted colours of this classic stoneware jar are a perfect foil for the lovely purple flowers of this primula.

Strength in Numbers

Plants in individual pots dotted around the room seldom look as effective as when they are grouped together. Even moving one piece of furniture to create a more integrated scene can make a great difference. Try it . . . you'll probably be surprised at the result.

1 All the individual plants here look good in their own right, but they don't look as though they have been arranged with thought.

By grouping plants and looking at the plants and furniture together, you can create stunning transformations.

2 Here the scattered plants on the windowsill have been placed in an attractive container.

3 Grouping the three plants on the chest of drawers in a basket has created more impact than before.

Light and Shade

You can use lighting – especially spotlights – to create different effects. The whole mood can be changed by the way you illuminate a plant. Be prepared to experiment to find the right effect.

Lighting from above will create hard and dramatic shadows. This will draw attention to the plant and it may be the effect you desire, but you may find the shadows distracting.

Lighting from below will make more of the container. Whether this is desirable or not depends on how attractive the container is. With some variegated foliage plants, illuminating more of the underside of the leaves can bring out markings and colourings that may otherwise go unnoticed.

Above: Back lighting can be very effective. It creates a sense of drama without distracting hard shadows. It highlights glossy leaves but may throw flowers into silhouette.

Left: The use of a mirror can be especially effective. Not only does it throw more light on to the plant, making more of the "dark" side of the plant, it also makes the plant look much larger.

Cheap and Cheerful

You don't have to spend a fortune on houseplants – you can raise dozens of plants for the cost of a packet of seeds and a bag of potting soil. Those requiring a long growing season in good light (such as cinerarias and calceolarias) are best raised in a greenhouse and brought inside when in bud. But plants like Busy Lizzies (impatiens) and Persian violets (exacums) can be raised and grown indoors on a windowsill that gets plenty of light.

MATERIALS AND TOOLS
2 pots
Crocks or chipped bark
Potting soil
Seeds
Sieve
Clear plastic bags

pot

clear plastic bags

GROWING ON

As soon as the seedlings are large enough to handle, prick (thin) them out into individual small pots. Holding the individual plant by a seed leaf (the first to open, which will probably be different in form from the subsequent leaves), insert it gently into a hole made in the potting soil in the new pot with a dibber or pencil. Try not to damage the roots or fragile stem, but gently firm the potting soil around the seedling. Water to settle it in.

1 Unless you plan to give a lot of seedlings away to friends, save space and sow a small number of seeds in a pot rather than filling a whole seed tray. Cover the drainage holes with crocks or chipped bark, then fill the pot with soil.

2 Firm down gently with the base of another pot to provide a level surface for sowing. The surface of the soil should be about 1 cm (½ in) below the rim of the pot.

3 Sprinkle the seeds as thinly and evenly as possible, between the fingers and thumb. If the seeds are very small, try mixing them with a little fine sand to make sowing easier.

4 Sift some potting soil or sand over the seeds, unless the packet instructs otherwise.

5 Stand the pot in a bowl of shallow water until moisture appears on the surface of the soil, then remove and allow to drain.

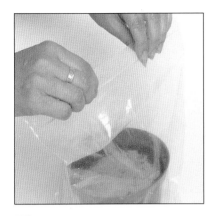

6 Enclose the pot in a plastic bag to conserve moisture, then set it in a light place out of direct sun. When seedlings germinate, remove the plastic bag and keep in a light position that is not too hot and sunny. Make sure the potting soil does not dry out.

CARE AND PROPAGATION

Sowing and Reaping

Buying all your houseplants can become expensive, but for the price of a packet of seeds and some potting soil you can grow dozens or even hundreds. Many short-term flowering houseplants – especially annuals – are easily raised from seed, but you can also buy the seeds of many perennial flowering and foliage houseplants. Raising some of your own plants from seed not only saves you money, but is much more satisfying too.

MATERIALS AND TOOLS
Seed tray or pot
Potting soil
Seeds
Sheet of stiff paper
Piece of cardboard
Propagator

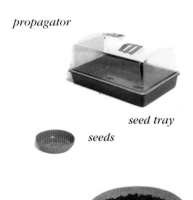

propagator

seed tray

seeds

potting soil

1 If you need very few plants, sow in a pot. If you want to germinate lots of seed, perhaps because you have a greenhouse or conservatory to grow them on in, or so that you can give some to friends, use a seed tray. Use a potting soil intended for seed-sowing, or a multi-purpose soil. Loosely fill the seed tray to just below the rim.

2 You may find it easier to distribute the seeds evenly if you tip them on to a piece of folded, stiff paper first.

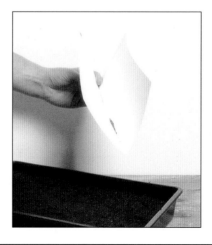

3 Scatter the seeds carefully and evenly over the surface, or tap the paper with a finger, as you move it over the surface, to release the seeds slowly.

4 Strike off the potting soil to level it and compress it slightly to eliminate the largest air pockets. You can improvise with a piece of wood or use strong cardboard like this.

5 Cover the seeds with more potting soil unless the instructions on the packet tell you not to do so (some germinate better if not covered). You can do this by hand if the seeds are large, but for a thin covering over fine seeds it is better to use a fine sieve to sift it over the surface.

6 Water with a fine rose or stand the tray or pot in a bowl of shallow water until dampness appears at the surface. Allow to drain, then place the tray in a propagator until the seeds germinate or the seedlings have to be potted up. If you don't have a propagator, cover the tray with a sheet of glass or plastic and keep in a warm place (such as an airing cupboard), but move them to a windowsill that gets plenty of light as soon as the first seed germinates.

HOUSEPLANTS TIP

Pot up the seedlings into individual pots as soon as they are large enough to handle, and before they become overcrowded and begin to compete with each other. Some plants will need potting on into larger pots several times before they reach flowering size or are large enough to make a good foliage display.

Soft and Easy

Many houseplants can be propagated from softwood cuttings, and these are particularly easy to root. Some will root in a week or two and there are usually soft new shoots suitable for the cuttings from early spring until late summer.

MATERIALS AND TOOLS
Pot
Potting soil
Plant with soft young growth
Secateurs (pruners)
Sharp knife
Hormone rooting powder or gel
Small dibber
3 small split canes
Clear plastic bag
Plastic-covered wire, or elastic band

1 Fill a pot with multi-purpose potting soil or a special cuttings mixture. Firm it down lightly.

2 Look on the plant for new growth at the tips that is still soft and bendy. The length of the cutting will depend on the plant, but usually 2.5–7.5 cm (1–3 in) is about right for most houseplants.

Tradescantia

pot

wire

clear plastic bag

dibber   *sharp knife*   *hormone rooting powder*   *secateurs (pruners)*

3 Trim the shoot neatly just below a leaf joint with a sharp knife. Remove the lowest pair of leaves.

4 Dip the cut end of the cutting into a hormone rooting powder, then tap off the excess. Alternatively, dip into a rooting gel.

5 Use a small dibber (a pencil will do if you don't have one) to make holes near the edge of the pot. Insert the cutting and firm in gently. Repeat with the rest of the cuttings. Water, then allow the pot to drain.

6 Once the cuttings have been inserted, place in a propagator or cover with a plastic bag. Insert small canes to keep the bag clear of the cuttings. Secure the bag in place with wire or an elastic band. Keep the pot in a light position out of direct sun. Check the bag daily and turn it inside out if there is very heavy condensation (some condensation for part of the day is normal).

GROWING ON

Pot up individually as soon as the cuttings have formed plenty of roots. You may be able to see roots appearing at the bottom of the pot, otherwise tip the ball of soil carefully out of the pot to check for roots once the cuttings seem to be making new growth.

Divide to Multiply

The easiest method of increasing your plants is to divide them: this will give you new plants instantly. Unfortunately, not all plants can be divided easily. The best ones for this technique have a crown with a number of stems arising from the base, and usually a mass of fibrous roots. If the plant forms a clump, it can usually be divided successfully.

MATERIALS AND TOOLS
Large clump-forming plant
Pots
Potting soil

Aglaonema

1 Always water the plant at least half an hour before dividing it; the compost will then be moist and so pulling it apart is less likely to damage the roots.

2 Remove the plant from its pot. You may find that you are able to pull the plant out with a gentle tug, otherwise invert the pot and tap the rim on a hard surface. This will usually loosen the root-ball.

3 Remove some of the soil, but try to avoid damaging the roots as much as possible. You should remove only enough to make it clear where the crown can be divided.

4 Separate the plant into pieces, making sure that each one has both roots and shoots.

5 The more pieces you divide it into, the smaller the new plants will be. If you require only one or two extra plants, simply divide it into two or three pieces.

6 Pot up the new plants immediately. Water in, then keep in a shaded position for a few days. Misting the plants with water several times a day will help them to re-establish quickly.

Here you have three plants instead of one. Although it may take several months, or even longer, for each piece to grow to the size of the original plant, you will end up with several plants for the price of one.

Turn Over a New Leaf

A few plants are really easy to propagate from individual leaves, including popular houseplants such as saintpaulias and some peperomias. As every healthy leaf is a potential new plant, you should have plenty to give to friends!

MATERIALS AND TOOLS
Suitable plant
Sharp knife
Pot
Potting soil
Small dibber
Propagator or plastic bag and
    elastic band

1 Choose a full-sized but fresh and healthy leaf and cut it from the plant with a length of stalk.

2 Fill a pot with a multi-purpose potting soil or cuttings mixture, then make a hole with a small dibber or a pencil before inserting the leaf stalk. The bottom of the blade of the leaf should just touch the surface of the soil. Insert all the cuttings.

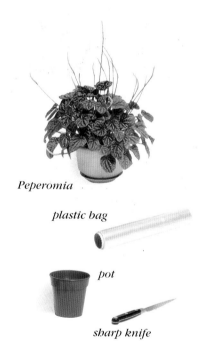

Peperomia

plastic bag

pot

sharp knife

3 Firm the cuttings gently, then water well. Allow to drain.

4 Place in a propagator if possible, otherwise cover with a plastic bag but ensure the sides do not come into contact with the leaves. Secure with an elastic band.

Leaf Slashing

Begonia rex can also be propagated from leaf cuttings, using a different technique. Select recently mature leaves that are healthy and vigorous.

MATERIALS AND TOOLS
Begonia rex
Sharp knife
Seed tray
Potting soil
Small pebbles
Propagator

Begonia rex leaf

sharp knife

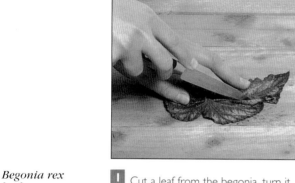

1 Cut a leaf from the begonia, turn it over and cut across the main veins with a sharp knife, making the cuts 2.5 cm (1 in) or more apart.

2 Lay the leaf flat on a tray of multi-purpose potting soil or cuttings mixture. Weight it down with small pebbles to keep it in contact with the soil. Keep in a humid atmosphere in a propagator until small plantlets can be seen growing from the cut veins. Pot them up into individual pots when they are large enough to handle comfortably.

Laying it Out

Layering can be used for a number of houseplants with creeping or prostrate stems. The most popular one is ivy, which roots easily and is a good choice for your first attempt at layering.

MATERIALS AND TOOLS
Small pots
Potting soil
Suitable plant
Pieces of bent wire

ivy

small pots

wire

1 Fill the pots with a multi-purpose potting soil or cuttings mixture, and firm down gently.

2 Separate out some young, vigorous stems long enough to be layered easily.

3 Peg the stems down into the potting soil, using the pieces of bent wire. The ideal position is 2.5 cm (1 in) or so back from the tip.

4 Remember to water regularly. Rooting is usually well established after a couple of weeks, and once the new plant is growing vigorously you can sever it from its parent.

Plants from the Air

Air-layering is not a practical way to raise a lot of new plants, but it is useful if you want just one or two, or if a plant like *Ficus elastica* has become bare at the base. You can air-layer the leafy top and start off again with a new, well-clothed plant.

MATERIALS AND TOOLS
Plastic bag or sheet
Suitable plant (see below)
Plastic-covered wire ties,
    or adhesive tape
Sharp knife
Matchstick
Hormone rooting powder
Sphagnum moss
Cane (stake) (optional)

Ficus elastica

plastic bag or sheet

sharp knife

1 Cut off a length of the plastic from the bag or sheet and secure it beneath the point where you want the roots to grow. Attach it with tape or a plastic-covered wire tie.

2 Using a very sharp knife, make an upward cut about 1 cm (¹/₂ in) long between two leaf joints. Be careful not to penetrate more than halfway through the stem, otherwise it may break off.

3 Keep the wound open with a small wedge such as a matchstick, and apply some hormone rooting powder to the wound. Pack a generous amount of damp moss, into which the roots will grow, around the wound.

WHAT TO LAYER, WHEN

The plant most often air-layered is the rubber plant (*Ficus elastica*), but you may be able to air-layer other tall, woody plants. The one we used to demonstrate the technique is still a young specimen well clothed with leaves. The method is normally used on old plants that have become bare at the base where the older leaves have fallen off.

4 Secure the plastic cover at the top, in order to enclose the ball of moss. If the top of the plant seems insecure, insert a cane (stake) and attach the top and bottom halves to this.

Winter Warnings

The cold days and nights of winter can bring trouble to houseplants, and prized plants may be lost that could otherwise be saved with a little forethought and a few precautions. Try these simple steps to cut down the losses.

Many of the tougher houseplants can be kept outside during the summer – it makes more room indoors, and the plants usually benefit from the experience provided you acclimatize them carefully first. They must be brought indoors well before the first frost, however. Clean up the pot, or, if you planted them in the open ground, pot them up again. Check for pests such as slugs and snails, and deal with any of these problems before you bring the plants inside.

In rooms where it is visually acceptable, such as a conservatory or perhaps a spare bedroom, insulate the window with bubble wrap. Cacti and succulents should be kept in good light all year round, but many benefit from a cold spell in winter provided the temperature remains above freezing.

The main risk to houseplants in winter often comes at night, as outside temperatures drop and the heating is perhaps turned down or even off. Even if the room is warm, if thick curtains are drawn at night the windowsill will become very cold. Remember to move your houseplants off the windowsill when you close the curtains.

Plants close to the window are especially vulnerable at night. You may be able to provide sufficient protection from the cold by placing expanded polystyrene tiles in front of the glass at night. Don't forget to remove the tiles in the morning.

Many plants will benefit from artificial light in winter Saintpaulias need it to keep flowering. Lights specially balanced for plant growth are best, but ordinary room lights are better than nothing. It needs to be close to the plant to be effective, but beware of placing a tungsten light too close because of the heat generated.

Creating a Microclimate

If your plants don't seem to be doing well, and they live in a hot, dry room, they may respond to a more humid atmosphere. You can achieve this by misting them frequently with water, but it's easier to create a humid microclimate for them. Grouping plants like this will also make more impact than having them dotted around the room.

1 Use a large, shallow tray and place fine gravel or expanded clay granules in the base. The layer must be thick enough to keep the bottom of the pots above the water that will stand in the base of the tray.

2 Arrange your plants on the tray. It doesn't matter if they are packed in closely, it all helps to create a better growing environment.

3 Water the plants normally, but don't worry if surplus water stands in the tray – provided it does not come above the top of the gravel. The water will gradually evaporate and create a humid atmosphere around the plants – just what most of them will appreciate.

4 You can help them along further by misting the leaves with water once or twice a day. Most plants will respond enthusiastically to this treatment.

Vacation Care

Going on vacation may not be good news for your houseplants if a friend or neighbour can't take care of the watering for you. But there are plenty of ways to help your plants through this period of potential stress.

Simply grouping plants together in a tray or large container will help. Water them thoroughly before you go away, and leave a little water in the bottom of the outer container. Don't worry if the bases of the pots are standing in a little water, provided it is not so deep that the potting soil will remain waterlogged for many days.

You can buy ceramic pot waterers that have a porous base through which the water from a small reservoir seeps for a period of days. Push the base into the pot and fill up with water. These are useful for one or two plants during a short holiday, but are not practical if you have a lot of plants.

Small plants can be placed in a plastic bag, sealed to maintain a humid atmosphere. The moisture condenses on the bag and runs down to be taken up by the plant again. This can be a useful technique for a few plants that do not mind this level of humidity.

Capillary wicks are available (you can also cut them from capillary matting) to draw water from a reservoir. Make sure the wicks are soaked and put deeply into the potting soil. The other end must reach the bottom of the reservoir. Water the plants thoroughly first.

A good way to keep your houseplants happy while you are away for a week is to buy a capillary mat (sold for greenhouse benches) and cut it to fit the drainer on your sink. Make sure you leave it long enough for the end to reach the bottom of the sink. Water the plants thoroughly and moisten the capillary mat. Make sure that one end of the mat reaches the bottom of the sink, then fill the sink with water. Moisture will be transferred to the plants by capillary action.

Index of Botanical and Common Names

Howea forsteriana syn. *Kentia forsteriana*
  (Kentia palm/Paradise palm)
Hoya (Wax flower/Common wax plant)
Hyacinthus (Hyacinth)
Hypocyrta glabra syn. *Nematanthus glaber*
  (Clog plant)
Hypoestes phyllostachya syn. *H. sanguinolenta*
  (Polka dot plant/Freckle face)
Impatiens (Busy Lizzie)
Jasminum (Jasmine)
Jasminum officinale (White jasmine)
Jasminum polyanthum (Pink jasmine)
Justicia brandegeeana syn. *Beloperone*
  guttata (Shrimp plant)
Kalanchoë blossfeldiana (Flaming Katy)
Kalanchoë daigremontiana syn. *Bryophyllum*
  daigremontianum (Devil's backbone)
Kalanchoë tubiflora syn. *Bryophyllum*
  tubiflorum (Chandelier plant)
Lilium (Lily)
Mammillaria (Nipple cactus/Pincushion
  cactus)
Mammillaria zeilmanniana (Rose pincushion)
Maranta (Prayer plant)
Miltonia (Pansy orchid)
Mimosa pudica (Sensitive plant)
Monstera deliciosa (Swiss cheese
  plant/Mexican breadfruit)
Narcissus (Daffodil)
Neoregelia carolinae syn. *Nidularium*
  carolinae (Blushing bromeliad)
Nephrolepis (Ladder fern)
Nephrolepis exaltata (Sword fern)
Nephrolepis exaltata 'Bostoniensis' (Boston
  fern)
Nephrolepis exaltata 'Whitmanii' (Lace fern)
Nerium oleander (Oleander)
Nertera granadensis syn. *N. depressa* (Bead
  plant)
Nidularium fulgens (Blushing bromeliad)
Opuntia (Prickly pear)
Opuntia microdasys (Bunny ears/Rabbit's ears)
Oxalis deppei (Lucky clover)
Pachystachys lutea (Lollipop plant)
Pelargonium (Geranium)
Pelargonium peltatum (Ivy-leaved geranium)
Pelargonium x domesticum (Regal
  pelargonium)
Pelargonium x zonale (Zonal pelargonium)

Pellaea rotundifolia (Button fern/New
  Zealand cliffbrake)
Pellaea viridis (Green brake fern)
Peperomia griseoargentea syn. *P. hederifolia*
  (Ivy peperomia)
Peperomia obtusifolia (Desert privet)
Peperomia verticillata (Whorled peperomia)
Philodendron bipinatifidum (Tree
  philodendron)
Philodendron erubescens (Blushing
  philodendron)
Philodendron scandens (Sweetheart plant)
Phoenix canariensis (Canary date palm)
Phoenix dactylifera (Date palm)
Phoenix roebelenii (Pygmy date palm)
Pilea cadierei (Aluminium plant)
Pilea microphylla (Artillery plant)
Platycerium bifurcatum (Stag's-horn fern)
Polyscias fruticosa (Dinner plate aralia)
Primula malacoides (Fairy primrose)
Primula vulgaris (Primrose)
Pteris (Ribbon fern)
Pteris cretica (Brake fern/Stove fern/Table
  fern)
Rhipsalidopsis gaertneri syn. *Schlumbergera*
  gaertneri (Easter cactus)
Rhododendron obtusum (Japanese azalea)
Rhododendron simsii (Indian azalea)
Rhoicissus capensis (Cape grape)
Rhoicissus rhomboidea (Grape ivy)
Saintpaulia (African violet)
Sansevieria trifasciata 'Laurentii' (Mother-in-
  law's tongue)
Sauromatum venosum syn. *S. guttatum*
  (Monarch-of-the-East/Voodoo lily)
Saxifraga stolonifera syn. *S. sarmentosa*
  (Mother of thousands/Strawberry
  geranium)
Schefflera actinophylla (Umbrella plant)
Schefflera arboricola syn. *Heptapleurum*
  arboricola (Parasol plant)

Schizanthus (Butterfly flower/Poor man's
  orchid)
Schlumbergera truncata syn. *Zygocactus*
  truncatus (Christmas cactus/Crab cactus)
Sedum (Stonecrop)
Sedum pachyphyllum (Jelly beans)
Senecio cruentus hybrids (Cineraria)
Sinningia speciosa (Gloxinia)
Smithiantha (Temple bells)
Solanum capsicastrum (Christmas
  cherry/Winter cherry/Jerusalem
  cherry/False   Jerusalem cherry)
Solanum pseudocapsicum (Christmas
  cherry/Winter cherry/Jerusalem cherry)
Soleirolia soleirolii syn. *Helxine soleirolii*
  (Baby's tears/Mind your own business)
Sparmannia africana (African hemp)
Spathiphyllum (Peace lily/Spathe flower)
Stephanotis floribunda (Madagascar
  jasmine/Wax flower/Common wax plant)
Strelitzia reginae (Bird of paradise flower)
Streptocarpus (Cape primrose)
Syngonium podophyllum (Arrowhead
  vine/Goosefoot plant)
Tillandsia (Air plant)
Tillandsia usneoides (Spanish moss)
Tolmeia menziesii (Pick-a-back
  plant/Piggyback plant)
Tradescantia (Wandering Jew/Inch plant)
Tulipa (Tulip)
Vriesea splendens (Flaming sword)
Washingtonia (Washington palm)
Yucca aloifolia (Spanish bayonet)
Yucca elephantipes (Spineless yucca)
Zygocactus truncatus syn. *Schlumbergera*
  truncata (Christmas cactus/Crab cactus)

Index